Write Fright

A Guide to Writing Scary Stories

Mark Pierce
Karen Jennings

Good Year Books
An Imprint of Pearson Learning

Dedication

To cousin Richard, a huge fan of horror; to Andy, Diane, and Harold; to Betty and Tom; to Bobbie Dempsey for inspiring the book; to Suzanne Beason, our wonderful editor; and to Alfred Hitchcock, Stephen King, and George Romero, our Write Fright role models.

Good Year Books
are available for most basic curriculum subjects plus many enrichment areas. For more Good Year Books, contact your local bookseller or educational dealer. For a complete catalog with information about other Good Year Books, please write:

Good Year Books
299 Jefferson Road
Parsippany, NJ 07054

Book Design: PenLine Productions
Cover Illustration: Wendy Edelson
Interior Illustrations: David Hohn
Design Manager: M. Jane Heelan
Editorial Manager: Suzanne Beason
Executive Editor: Judith Adams

This Book Is Printed
on Recycled Paper

About Write Fright

Children love experiences that give them the creeps, grip them in suspense, or make them scream. They shriek gleefully during scary rides at the amusement park. They giggle nervously during games of hide and seek. They sit in rapt attention listening to tales of terror. They learn early on that a good scare is invigorating wherever it comes from.

Ghost stories, horror movies, and weird true tales have captured the imagination of children for generations, and young readers today have an even wider selection of thrills and chills to choose from. They can fill their bookshelves with selections from *Goosebumps* or any of the other juvenile novels designed to demonstrate the power of the mysterious to surprise and delight. The demand for this kind of fiction is resoundingly high, as children anxiously seek out writing that frightens.

This youthful affinity for horror is more than mere child's play. Chill- and thrill-seeking serves a valuable developmental function by encouraging the young to process their anxieties in a way that's healthy. They hear and read tales of horror to discover and enjoy what is unknown about the world they live in.

Horror stories allow their readers to venture into an innovative realm, a place where nothing is what it seems to be, and anything can happen. It is a place filled with mystery and suspense, humor and excitement. Horror has it all.

Write Fright capitalizes on students' natural and healthy enjoyment of scary tales and encourages them to become writers themselves.

The exercises in *Write Fright* incorporate creative writing fundamentals such as conflict, use of action verbs, descriptive writing, similes, metaphors, alliteration, character description, sensory imagery, onomatopoeia, genres, how to develop characters, brainstorming, rewriting, and the importance of who, what, when, where, and why in fiction writing.

Write Fright features numerous story starters designed to spark the imagination of even the most reluctant writers, and ideas to inspire them from myths, parables, and the writing of Edgar Allan Poe.

We have tried to appeal to children's unwavering interest in monsters, vampires, scientists, animal transformations, haunted houses, and what happens when the clock strikes midnight. We have purposely avoided the use of violence or ideas that are inappropriately macabre. Many of the exercises are designed to be both humorous and scary.

Write Fright capitalizes on students' love of the creepy, kooky, and scary to strengthen their writing skills and inspire them creatively.

What more could any kid hope for?

What more could any teacher dream of?

Mark Pierce
Karen Jennings

Table of Contents

Write Fright, Copyright © Good Year Books.

Introduction

Presenting the Exercises

The first three chapters of this book explore the concepts and techniques writers use to create memorable scary stories. Once they become aware of the techniques used in horror story writing, students proceed to exercises involving story starters and rewriting. The level of complexity of the exercises increases somewhat as the book progresses, and the skills acquired in earlier exercises can be applied to later writing assignments.

It is not necessary to approach the exercises in this book as a step-by-step process. They may be viewed as a variety of writing suggestions. The teacher or writer may choose either to present or do the exercises in any order, jumping back and forth to develop and/or improve a story or proceed in the order the book is presented, whichever best meets the needs of the individual writer or class.

Keeping a Portfolio

Write Fright includes a chapter about rewriting and many of the writing skills exercises can be used for rewriting stories. By having your young writers maintain a portfolio, you can encourage them to improve on their stories.

With a portfolio, a student can keep his or her stories organized into different drafts. The student can use different activities as springboards for revisiting and reworking earlier drafts.

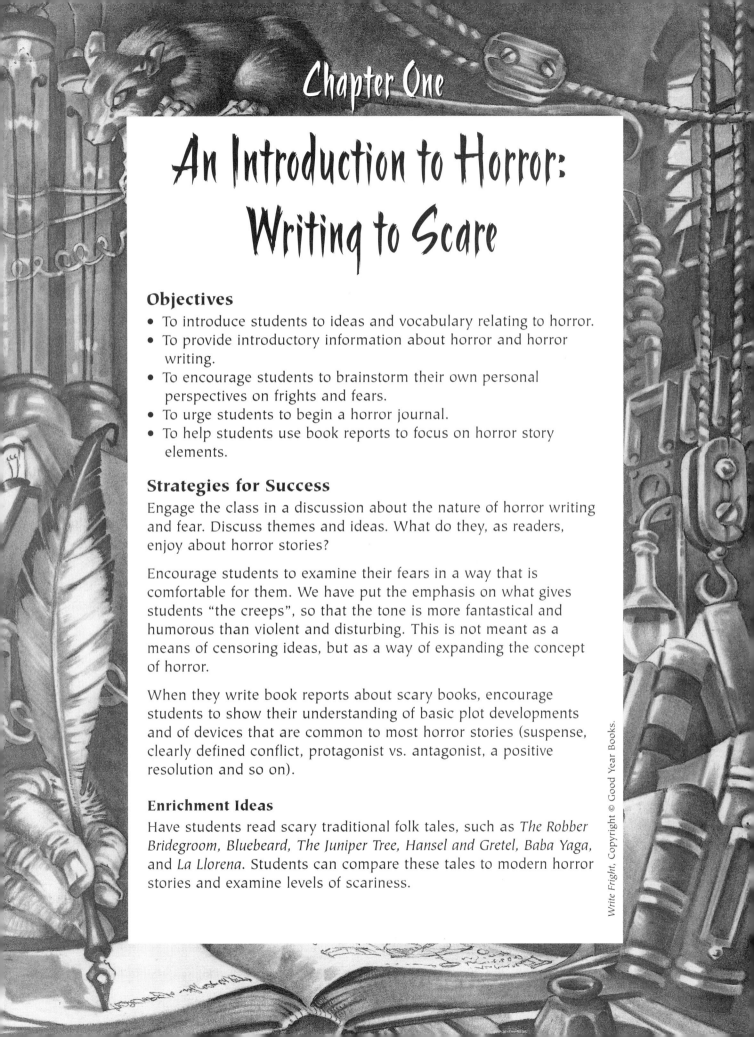

Chapter One

An Introduction to Horror: Writing to Scare

Objectives

- To introduce students to ideas and vocabulary relating to horror.
- To provide introductory information about horror and horror writing.
- To encourage students to brainstorm their own personal perspectives on frights and fears.
- To urge students to begin a horror journal.
- To help students use book reports to focus on horror story elements.

Strategies for Success

Engage the class in a discussion about the nature of horror writing and fear. Discuss themes and ideas. What do they, as readers, enjoy about horror stories?

Encourage students to examine their fears in a way that is comfortable for them. We have put the emphasis on what gives students "the creeps", so that the tone is more fantastical and humorous than violent and disturbing. This is not meant as a means of censoring ideas, but as a way of expanding the concept of horror.

When they write book reports about scary books, encourage students to show their understanding of basic plot developments and of devices that are common to most horror stories (suspense, clearly defined conflict, protagonist vs. antagonist, a positive resolution and so on).

Enrichment Ideas

Have students read scary traditional folk tales, such as *The Robber Bridegroom*, *Bluebeard*, *The Juniper Tree*, *Hansel and Gretel*, *Baba Yaga*, and *La Llorena*. Students can compare these tales to modern horror stories and examine levels of scariness.

Hey, Dr. Jekyll, No Need to Hide: Facing Your Fears

Most horror authors write about things they find scary—things like ghosts, snakes, monsters, aliens, weird transformations or sudden surprises. As you begin your journey into the land of horror, look at what frightens you. Then you can use these basic fears in your writing.

1. **List five things that give you the creeps.**

    _____

    _____

    _____

    _____

    _____

    _____

    _____

    _____

    _____

    _____

2. **Of these top five, which one scares you the most? Describe your feelings about this fear.**

    _____

    _____

    _____

    _____

    _____

    _____

    _____

    _____

    _____

    _____

3. Describe the scariest place you have ever been.

_____

_____

_____

_____

_____

_____

_____

_____

_____

_____

_____

4. Describe the scariest dream you have ever had.

_____

_____

_____

_____

_____

_____

_____

_____

_____

_____

_____

5. What is fear?

_____

_____

_____

_____

_____

_____

_____

_____

_____

_____

_____

_____

My Favorite Scares:
Starting a Horror Journal

It's a great idea to begin a horror journal. You can record all of your frightening thoughts and ideas. Your journal can be a place for you to write stories, collect or draw pictures, and describe your research into what people find frightening. That is what this next exercise is for. Write about what scares other people. You'll discover more about universal fears—fears that are held by most people.

1. **What scares your parents and teachers?**

_____

_____

_____

_____

_____

_____

_____

_____

_____

_____

2. **What scares your friends?**

_____

_____

_____

_____

_____

_____

_____

_____

_____

_____

3. What scares really young children? Hint: Think about what *you* were afraid of when you were little.

_____

_____

_____

_____

_____

_____

_____

_____

_____

_____

_____

4. On a separate sheet of paper, use your ideas to write a story called

The Town That Was Afraid of Everything

You Must Remember This: Past Frights

Now you are going to examine what other writers, directors, and storytellers have created that have had a lasting impact on you. Their ideas can inspire you as you create your own successful scares.

1. **What is the scariest story you have every heard? Describe it.**

_____

_____

_____

_____

_____

_____

_____

_____

_____

_____

2. **What is your favorite scary movie? Describe it.**

_____

_____

_____

_____

_____

_____

_____

_____

_____

_____

3. What is your favorite scary television show? Describe it.

_____

_____

_____

_____

_____

_____

_____

_____

_____

_____

_____

4. What is your favorite scary book? Describe it.

_____

_____

_____

_____

_____

_____

_____

_____

_____

_____

_____

_____

_____

_____

Words to Learn:
A Ghastly Vocabulary

Below is a list of some eerie and descriptive vocabulary words. You will find them useful in your writing. Use each word in a sentence. Look up the words you don't know.

1. terrified _____

_____

2. ominous _____

_____

3. unearthly _____

_____

4. suspense _____

_____

5. dreadful _____

_____

6. dreary _____

_____

7. mysterious _____

_____

8. ghastly _____

_____

9. terror _____

_____

10. horrendous _____

_____

11. **apprehensive** _____

_____

12. **writhing** _____

_____

13. **aberrant** _____

_____

14. **ooze** _____

_____

15. **misty** _____

_____

16. **wretched** _____

_____

17. **shock** _____

_____

18. **horror** _____

_____

19. **suspicious** _____

_____

20. **baleful** _____

_____

Learning From Other Authors: Writing Reports on Frightful Books

Scary books have always been very popular. Since you are going to learn how to write scary stories, take a look at how other authors have gone about writing some terrific tales of terror. Ask your teacher or librarian to recommend a scary novel. Read it. Then answer the following questions.

What is the title and author of the book?

_____

How does this book begin? Does it start scary? Is there a sense that something is going to go wrong?

_____

_____

_____

_____

_____

When does the terror begin? Does it jump out at you or does it build slowly?

_____

_____

_____

_____

_____

How does the story end?

_____

_____

_____

_____

_____

Describe the main characters. Were there protagonists and antagonists in the tale?

_____

_____

_____

_____

_____

_____

_____

_____

_____

_____

_____

What did you like best about the book?

_____

_____

_____

_____

_____

_____

_____

_____

_____

_____

_____

_____

_____

What Do You Think?: Freewriting About Horror

Most people enjoy a good scare...at least occasionally! It gives a sense of relief. When you ride a roller coaster, you are thrilled and frightened. When the ride is over, you're relieved and excited. That's what a real fright does for you. It's called the "Boo! Phew!" response. Horror writers use this response to keep readers on the edge of their seats. They use imaginary events to work you up. For this exercise, think of the last horror movie you saw that really scared you. Write down your thoughts about being scared. Let your mind and pen flow.

Thrills and Chills I Remember

_____

_____

_____

_____

_____

_____

_____

_____

_____

_____

_____

_____

_____

_____

_____

_____

_____

_____

_____

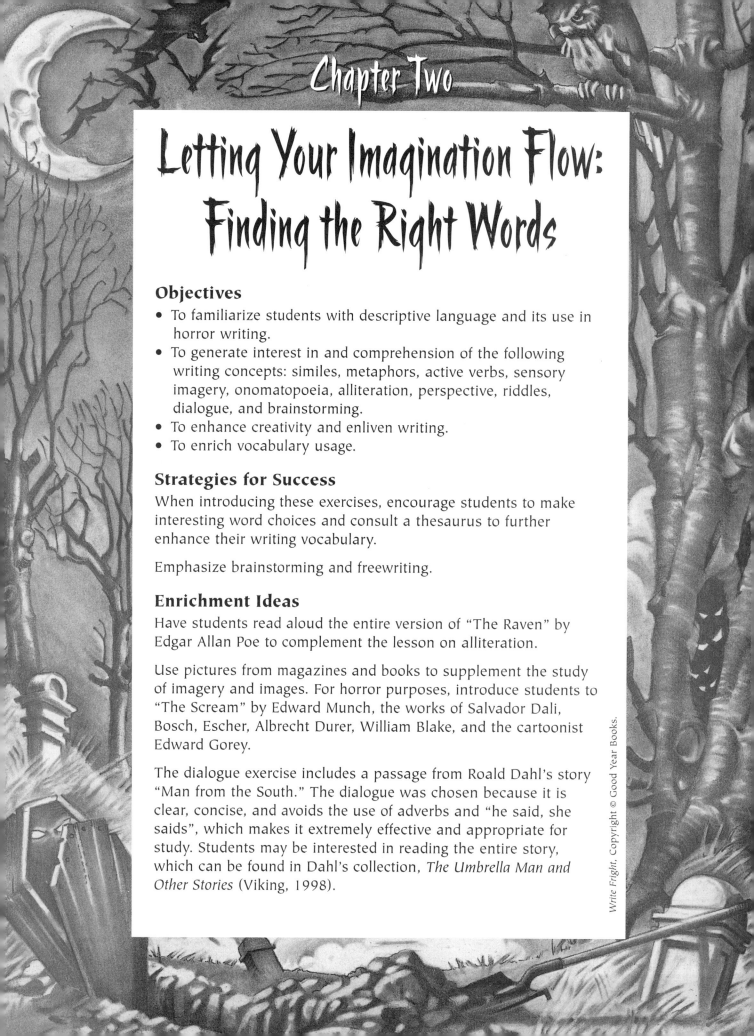

Chapter Two

Letting Your Imagination Flow: Finding the Right Words

Objectives

- To familiarize students with descriptive language and its use in horror writing.
- To generate interest in and comprehension of the following writing concepts: similes, metaphors, active verbs, sensory imagery, onomatopoeia, alliteration, perspective, riddles, dialogue, and brainstorming.
- To enhance creativity and enliven writing.
- To enrich vocabulary usage.

Strategies for Success

When introducing these exercises, encourage students to make interesting word choices and consult a thesaurus to further enhance their writing vocabulary.

Emphasize brainstorming and freewriting.

Enrichment Ideas

Have students read aloud the entire version of "The Raven" by Edgar Allan Poe to complement the lesson on alliteration.

Use pictures from magazines and books to supplement the study of imagery and images. For horror purposes, introduce students to "The Scream" by Edward Munch, the works of Salvador Dali, Bosch, Escher, Albrecht Durer, William Blake, and the cartoonist Edward Gorey.

The dialogue exercise includes a passage from Roald Dahl's story "Man from the South." The dialogue was chosen because it is clear, concise, and avoids the use of adverbs and "he said, she saids", which makes it extremely effective and appropriate for study. Students may be interested in reading the entire story, which can be found in Dahl's collection, *The Umbrella Man and Other Stories* (Viking, 1998).

Onomatopoeia:
What Was That Sound?

Onomatopoeia is a tool used by writers to describe sounds to their audience. The words imitate the sounds they are naming. Onomatopoeia is a great way for horror writers to create suspense and atmosphere.

Here are some examples of onomatopoeia

The door on the old Wilson house creaked and squeaked when I opened it.

The children screamed as they heard the boom and crash of the fireworks.

Now it's your turn to be onomatopoetic! Write about some of the sounds you hear using onomatopoeia to describe each setting or situation.

Here's an example: A busy highway:

The engines hummed and the tires whirred as the cars whizzed by on the freeway. Horns honked, blaring beep beep beep behind an old car that clanked and sputtered down the road.

a terrifying thunderstorm

_____

_____

_____

_____

_____

a pet store

_____

_____

_____

_____

a circus

_____

_____

_____

_____

_____

_____

_____

_____

a birthday party

_____

_____

_____

_____

_____

_____

_____

_____

_____

a busy kitchen

_____

_____

_____

_____

_____

_____

_____

_____

_____

Alliteration:
Words That Sneak Up on One Another

Alliteration is a descriptive tool that adds musicality to writing. When you hear the same sound at the beginning of two or more words, you are listening to alliteration.

For example:

The ghostly ghouls gave me gooseflesh.

The hand held us in horror.

Below is a classic example of scary alliteration. It is an excerpt from the poem "The Raven," written by one of the most famous horror authors, Edgar Allan Poe. Read it and circle all of the alliteration you can find. Hint: Reading it aloud will help you hear the alliteration more clearly.

The Raven
by Edgar Allan Poe

Once upon a midnight dreary, while I pondered, weak and weary,

Over many a quaint and curious volume of forgotten lore—

While I nodded, nearly napping, suddenly there came a tapping,

As of someone gently rapping, rapping at my chamber door.

"Tis some visitor," I muttered, "tapping at my chamber door—

        Only this and nothing more."

Deep into that darkness peering, long I stood there wondering, fearing,

Doubting, dreaming dreams no mortals ever dared to dream before;

But the silence was unbroken, and the stillness gave no token,

And the only word there spoken was the whispered word, "Lenore!"

This I whispered, and an echo murmured back the word, "Lenore!"—

        Merely this and nothing more.

Name _____ Date _____

Now, write your own poem. Be sure to include some alliteration. You may want to go to your library and read the complete version of "The Raven." Ask your librarian for assistance if you need help.

_____

_____

_____

_____

_____

_____

_____

_____

_____

_____

_____

_____

_____

_____

_____

_____

_____

_____

_____

_____

_____

_____

_____

_____

_____

_____

Write Fright, Copyright © Good Year Books.

Making Comparisons: Sink Your Teeth Into Similes

Comparisons can add a creative edge to your horror tales. A simile is a comparison of two unlike things that uses the word *like* or *as*.

For example:

She was so nervous, her heart was beating like a drum.

She was as nervous as a deer during hunting season.

Use similes to describe dread, horror, or fear and complete the sentences below. Then write two of your own.

1. Her **hands were shaking like** _____

2. Her **body was trembling like** _____

3. His **body was frozen like** _____

4. His **heart was pounding like** _____

5. His **knees were knocking like** _____

6. His _____ was _____ like _____

7. Her _____ was _____ like _____

Use similes to complete the sentences below. Then write two of your own.

1. I **was as scared as** _____

2. I **was as worried as** _____

3. I **was as frantic as** _____

4. I **was as terrified as** _____

5. I **was as relieved as** _____

6. I **was as weak as** _____

Monster Similes: Comparing Characteristics

Similes can be used to describe characteristics and emotions.

For example:

Wolfman's hair was as matted as a shag carpet.

Dracula's skin was as green as a ripe avocado.

In the spaces below, use similes to describe the characteristics of classic horror characters.

1. Frankenstein's neck bolts were as _____

   as _____.

2. Dracula's fangs were as _____

   as _____.

3. The sea monster's scales were like _____

   _____.

4. The zombie's clothes were like _____

   _____.

5. The alien's body was like _____

   _____.

6. The werewolf's howl was like _____

   _____.

7. The mummy's bandages were like _____

   _____.

You can also use similes in your scary writing to add dimension, humor, and perspective.

For example:

Frankenstein's hands were as big as 10 pound lobsters but, compared to King Kong's, they looked like little goldfish.

Dracula's fangs were as long as knives, but compared to the Wolfman's, they looked like toothpicks.

Fill in the blanks below to make some more clever comparisons.

8. The Cyclops' _____ was/were as _____ as _____, but compared to _____ it/they looked like _____.

9. The Dancing Skeleton's _____ was/were as _____ as _____, but compared to _____ they looked like _____.

10. The Giant Worm's _____ was/were as _____ as _____, but compared to _____ they looked like _____.

It's Fair to Compare: Halloween Metaphors

Metaphors do not use the words *like* or *as* to compare two things. A metaphor is a figure of speech. It is a word or phrase that ordinarily conveys one thing but is used to convey another.

For example:

Snow is God's dandruff.

Life is just a bowl of cherries.

Metaphors add excitement to writing. They connect imaginative images to real concepts and ideas. Life isn't really a bowl of cherries, is it? But saying "life is just a bowl of cherries" is a more interesting way of saying, "life can be wonderful."

For this exercise, you are going to write metaphors about the scariest day of the year, Halloween.

Here are some examples:

Halloween is dress-up time.

Halloween is ghosting and ghouling from *door to door*.

Halloween is carnivals and candy.

Brainstorm your thoughts and feelings about Halloween. What does Halloween make you think of?

_____

_____

_____

_____

_____

_____

_____

_____

Now, write a metaphor poem about Halloween.

Halloween is . . .

_____

_____

_____

_____

_____

_____

_____

_____

_____

_____

_____

_____

_____

_____

_____

_____

_____

_____

_____

_____

_____

_____

_____

_____

_____

_____

_____

_____

Action Verbs: The Creature Slithered Along the Wall and I Shrieked!

Action verbs make writing come alive for the reader. The action verbs *run, scream, fly, crouch, hit, jump, sprint,* and *slither* are often used in horror stories. They add energy to the story and keep you on the edge of your seat. By using action verbs, you energize your writing. Read this sentence: *Tony was frightened of the zombies.* Now read this sentence: *Tony screamed in terror when he saw the zombies approaching.* Which one has more energy?

Change the underlined phrases in the sentences below to phrases containing action verbs.

1. The zombies <u>were headed</u> this way. _____

   _____

2. Steve <u>was leaving</u> the haunted house quickly. _____

   _____

3. Mrs. Weymeir <u>was hiding</u> in her closet. _____

   _____

4. The fog <u>was moving</u> towards the school. _____

   _____

5. The alien <u>was leaving</u> his spaceship. _____

   _____

6. The streetlights <u>were turning</u> on and off. _____

   _____

7. The wolf <u>was looking</u> at the old man. _____

   _____

Seeing Is Believing:
The Images of Suspense

Writers make comparisons with language. They use powerful images or pictures to convey meaning. Look around. What images do you see? Maybe you see other students writing, an open door, a dusty furnace, a kitchen table, or a sun-filled window.

Make a list of five things you see.

_____

_____

_____

_____

_____

_____

_____

_____

_____

_____

_____

On a separate sheet of paper, write a story about what would happen if all of the things you see suddenly went out of control. For example: *The students couldn't stop writing because their pens were moving at 70 miles per hour. The window began to open and shut by itself.* Title your story:

I Thought My Eyes Were Playing Tricks on Me

The Birds Seem to Know: Using the Sights and Sounds of Nature

Using nature in horror stories can be a valuable tool in building suspense and enhancing atmosphere or plot. In tales of horror, nature can become an active participant in the story.

For example:

A thick fog crept across the bay. An owl on the roof screamed an eerie warning as Joe turned the key in the lock.

Write a list of sights, sounds, and creatures in nature that you could use in a scary story.

_____

_____

_____

_____

_____

_____

_____

_____

Next, write a few descriptive sentences using some of the sights or sounds on your list.

_____

_____

_____

_____

_____

_____

_____

_____

Now write an introduction to a scary story. Use the elements of nature from your list and sentences to create the atmosphere and a sense of foreboding.

The Warning

_____

_____

_____

_____

_____

_____

_____

_____

_____

_____

_____

_____

_____

_____

_____

_____

_____

_____

_____

_____

_____

_____

_____

_____

_____

_____

Be Careful What You Wish For: A Reason For Conflict

Have you ever heard the expression "Be careful what you wish for. It might come true"? It has been said that horror fiction is about a writer facing his or her subconscious mind. Often, the danger in a horror story has been created by the main character's inner desires or wants.

Write a list of things you want. They can be serious, strange, or funny.

_____

_____

_____

_____

_____

_____

Choose one of the desires listed above, and brainstorm some of the possible side effects or consequences of the desire becoming a reality. Write your ideas in the space below.

_____

_____

_____

_____

_____

Use your list and ideas to write a story about how your character gets what he or she desires, but with shocking results. Title your story:

I Want It! I Want It!

Describing the Creature: Riddle Me This

Here is a first-person narrative in the form of a riddle.

Can you guess who this is from the description?

> I'm seven feet tall. I have a flat head. My skin is pale green. The only jewelry I wear is the bolts in my neck. My suit is torn because it doesn't fit me quite right. If you met me, you might scream, and I wouldn't know what to say. I'm afraid of fire. I was the result of an experiment gone wrong.
>
> Who am I?

This is your friend and mine, the Frankenstein monster.

Pick four of your favorite horror story characters. Write a first-person narrative riddle for each character, using the example above to guide you.

Riddle #1

_____

_____

_____

_____

_____

_____

_____

_____

_____

_____

Character's name: _____

Name _____ Date _____

Riddle #2

_____

_____

_____

_____

_____

_____

Character's name: _____

Riddle #3

_____

_____

_____

_____

_____

_____

Character's name: _____

Riddle #4

_____

_____

_____

_____

_____

_____

Character's name: _____

Late at Night My Thoughts Are Different: Brainstorming the Midnight Mind

We all think different thoughts depending upon what time of day it is. When we first wake up, we think about breakfast and the day ahead. When night falls, different thoughts occupy our minds. When writing a horror story, tap into your midnight mind. The ideas you find there can become part of your writer's bag of tricks.

Write down the thoughts you have late at night. Include your dreams, the noises you hear, and what you think might be lurking in the darkness. Fill up the entire page with your ideas.

My Midnight Thoughts

_____

_____

_____

_____

_____

_____

_____

_____

_____

_____

_____

_____

_____

_____

_____

_____

_____

_____

You Bet You Can: Writing Dialogue

Dialogue is the conversation between characters. Dialogue should be specific to each character. It should also advance the plot of a story. Many writers develop their skill at writing dialogue by writing down real conversations. As a result, their writing has the ring of truth. Good suspense writers use dialogue effectively. For example, Roald Dahl uses dialogue to advance the main plot in his tale "Man from the South." Read the following passage.

"You strike lighter successfully 10 times running and Cadillac is yours. You like to have dis Cadillac, yes?"

"Sure, I'd like to have Cadillac." The boy was still grinning.

"All right. Fine. We make a bet and I put up my Cadillac."

"And what do I put up?"

The little man carefully removed the red band from his still unlighted cigar. "I never ask you, my friend, to bet something you cannot afford. You understand?"

"Then what do I bet?"

"I make it very easy for you, yes?"

"OK. You make it easy."

"Some small ting you can afford to give away, and if you did happen to lose it you would not feel too bad. Right?"

"Such as what?'

"Such as, perhaps, de little finger on your left hand."

"My *what?*" The boy stopped grinning.

"Yes. Why not? You win, you take de car. You looss, I take de finger."

"I don't get it. How d'you mean, you take the finger?'

"I chop it off."

"Jumping jeepers! That's a crazy bet."

Imagine two characters who are making a crazy dare. Begin by brainstorming some ideas. Write your ideas in the space below.

_____

_____

_____

_____

_____

_____

_____

_____

_____

_____

_____

_____

_____

_____

_____

_____

_____

_____

_____

_____

_____

_____

_____

On a separate sheet of paper, use your brainstorming ideas to write the actual dialogue. See if you can write your dialogue *without* using the phrases "he said" and "she said." Let the conversation between the characters flow naturally. Include bits of action within the dialogue.

The Odor of Fear:
Using Your Sense of Smell and Touch

Use the senses of smell and touch to add a lot to the atmosphere of your scary tale. It's a surefire way to give your readers the creeps.

For example:

Susan knelt down and ran her fingers over the cold, wet gravestone. She knew the name engraved on the stone—William James. She went to his bakery every week with her mother until last summer, when he passed away. As she touched the stone, she gasped. The warm, pleasant odor of cookies filled the air. It was chocolatey and sweet. It was the same smell she noticed whenever she visited Mr. James' bakery. She turned and ran.

Scary, huh? Even the smell of chocolate chip cookies can be scary!

To awaken your sense of smell and touch, describe the following:

a fast food restaurant

_____

_____

_____

_____

_____

_____

_____

_____

_____

_____

_____

_____

Write Fright, Copyright © Good Year Books.

the woods after a rainstorm

_____

_____

_____

_____

_____

_____

_____

a favorite perfume

_____

_____

_____

_____

_____

_____

_____

_____

_____

an outdoor barbecue

_____

_____

_____

_____

_____

_____

_____

_____

_____

The Story of Dead Aaron: Using Sensory Imagery

Writers often use sensory imagery to describe people, places, or things. By doing so, their writing becomes more specific and vivid. When describing characters, you can explore their smell, feel, look, and the sound of their voice. Now, read the tale below about Dead Aaron.

The Tale of Dead Aaron

adapted by M. Pierce and K. Jennings

Aaron Kelly was wicked and old

Folks steered clear of him, so I'm told.

He was so mean that the day he died,

He came back from the other side.

He walked home from the cemetery,

To have dinner with his wife Mary.

Mary and the mourners stared with dread,

"What'cha doing Aaron? Don't you know you're dead?"

Aaron said, "Don't tell me what I am!

Now get out of my house! All you scram.

Calling me dead, when I feel fine.

Kinda cold in the joints, but I don't mind."

Mary was upset with Aaron's return,

"You don't belong here, when will you learn?"

He said, "Right here I'm gonna stay,

right here all night and all day.

Put a log on the fire cause I'm mighty cold."

And Aaron sat there and started to mold.

His bones cracked and his skin turned green,

But Aaron would not move—he was mighty mean.

Mary shared her house with this bag of bones,

Old Dead Aaron wouldn't let her alone.

She asked her friends everywhere,

how to get Aaron out of there.

Folks said, "Aaron's a mighty jealous man,

You should start dating, having fun again.

When Aaron sees you acting just like you're single

He'll fall apart like an old weathered shingle."

So Mary had a fella to her house for a meal,

Aaron tried to act like it was no big deal.

That evening their friend, the fiddler came by,

And started to fiddle as the moon filled the sky.

Aaron heard the music and he started to dance,

Mary thought, "Maybe this is my chance."

She told the fiddler, "Play quick, faster I say!"

Aaron spun around, some bones flew away.

He swung a big circle, his dry bones a-cracking,

A finger flew off, and his body went a-snapping.

Mary told the fiddler, "Play on, play on!"

Knowing directly Aaron would be gone.

In a snap, what was Aaron flew everywhere,

A bone landed here and a bone over there.

Mary took what was left back to his grave,

and mixed them all up this and that a way.

Aaron won't come back, maybe forever,

Because she made sure he couldn't put himself together.

Sometimes in his grave folks hear a clacking sound

It's Aaron's bones trying to dance all around.

But he never came back, folks don't think he can,

And Mary never found herself another man.

Write a character description of Dead Aaron using sensory imagery. Describe his looks, feel, sound, and smell.

_____

_____

_____

_____

_____

_____

_____

_____

_____

_____

_____

Next, write a sensory description of Aaron as a young man.

_____

_____

_____

_____

_____

_____

_____

_____

_____

_____

_____

Chapter Three

Putting The Pieces Together: Fear-Inducing Fundamentals

Objectives

- To encourage students to consider and develop the <u>who</u>, <u>what</u>, <u>where</u>, <u>when</u>, and <u>why</u> of horror writing.
- To introduce students to the technique of using magazine cut-outs and looking to other outside sources to gather story ideas.
- To strengthen students' story-writing skills.
- To emphasize research skills in story writing.

Strategies for Success

Review <u>who</u>, <u>what</u>, <u>where</u>, <u>when</u> and <u>why</u> in story writing as an introduction to this chapter. Discuss how these five elements would be used to write a compelling scary story.

Introduce the class to writing as an exploration. Many writers draw their ideas from articles in newspapers or actual events in their lives or neighbors' lives.

Several exercises in this chapter call for the use of magazines for gathering ideas. Have students bring old magazines to class for this purpose.

The random act of picking a picture idea from an envelope is a great way to get young writers over their fear of writing and enhances creativity. You can either use the magazine picture ideas we have included, or brainstorm lists of concepts and ideas before students begin writing; choose those at random.

Enrichment Ideas

Some of the exercises in this chapter would be enhanced with research. Research is one of the most important aspects of good fictional writing. To reinforce this idea, choose a fictional book from the library—one that the class might know and one that would have demanded some author research. Talk about the book. How was research involved in the writing of the book? Talk about how different the book would have been if the author had not done any research.

Write Fright, Copyright © Good Year Books.

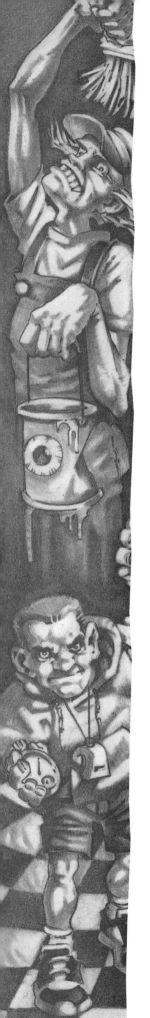

What Is It?: The Magazine Monster

Don't throw that magazine away! There's a monster in there! Really!

That magazine is like a monster egg waiting to hatch, and you are going to hatch it. You will create the first monster of its kind—ever. Here's how.

Look through some old magazines. Cut out pictures of people, products, and images that draw your interest. Cut those pictures into smaller images and glue them onto a piece of construction paper. Don't have anything in mind. Just paste and see what happens. As you paste on more and more, begin to think of your picture as a monster. What monster could this be? Start to build a monster out of the pieces that you have cut from magazines. Don't stop until what you have scares you. Then write a biography of your monster using who, what, where, when, and why.

Who is your monster? Give it a name.

_____

_____

_____

_____

_____

_____

_____

Where does your monster come from? Where does it live now?

_____

_____

_____

_____

_____

_____

_____

What does your monster eat? Why does it eat that? When does it eat?

_____

_____

_____

_____

_____

_____

Why did your monster come into being?

_____

_____

_____

_____

_____

_____

What does your monster do on a typical day?

_____

_____

_____

_____

_____

_____

Who knows your monster better than anyone? Describe this person.

_____

_____

_____

_____

_____

_____

What? and Why?: Oh No! It's a Big Hairy Monster! With Lipstick on?

A monster is ripping through the city. It is destroying cars and thrashing trees and buildings to pieces. For no good reason? No. There has to be a reason. Even monsters want something. But what? That is the question you are going to answer. What does your monster want?

Grab a stack of magazines. Cut out pictures of everything. *Everything, that is, except people and animals.* Put the pictures in an envelope, mix them up, and pick one. (Save the rest for later.) What have you picked? Let's say you picked—lipstick! That is what your monster wants. "Lipstick! No!" you scream. Yes, lipstick. But why? You tell me. Perhaps your monster has a date on Friday night and really needs something to make that night special. Maybe your monster needs lipstick to survive. Something about the chemical compound makes lipstick an essential vitamin in your monster's diet.

Once you know what your monster wants, your story can start to take shape. Your main character, or hero, must look beyond the destructive nature of your beast and figure out what the monster wants. But how will your hero figure that out? On a separate sheet of paper, write a story about the item you picked.

Stay Back! I Have a Chocolate Bar!: Finding the Fatal Flaw

Most characters in horror stories have fatal flaws that the protagonists can use against them. Sunlight and garlic will destroy Dracula. Daybreak makes the Werewolf return to human form. Water was all it took to take the Wicked Witch of the West down. This exercise is all about exposing *your* monster's weakness.

Go to your envelope with magazine pictures and pick out an item. (See page 42.) This time what you pull out will be deadly to your monster, like kryptonite is to Superman. Let's say you picked chocolate. Chocolate?!

Chocolate is deadly to your monster. Well, at least you know how to stop the monster. But wait—there's a problem. Your hero is also allergic to the same substance. He or she can't even touch it. So many problems, so little time! Now, using a separate sheet of paper, write a story titled:

The Weird Weakness

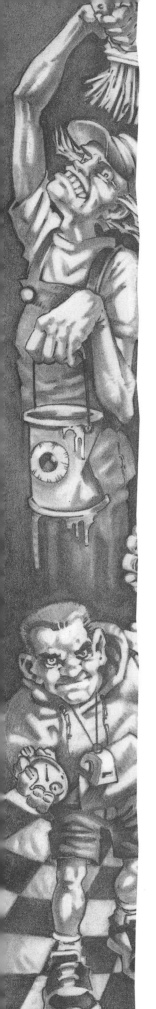

My Hero:
Who Will Save Us All?

In tales of horror, a hero is sometimes needed to save the day. The hero can be a clever student, a scientific expert, a teacher, a detective, or anyone at all. The hero is the enterprising protagonist who encounters the ghastly antagonist—and triumphs. You are going to create your own horror story hero.

Pull out that collection of pictures that you cut out of the magazines. (See page 42.) To complete the following sentences, pick out a picture and write down what you choose. Then complete the sentence that follows for each category.

1. **My hero really likes** _____

   He likes it because _____

   _____

   _____

   _____

   _____

2. **My hero really wants** _____

   He wants it because _____

   _____

   _____

   _____

   _____

3. **My hero really dislikes** _____

   He can't stand it because _____

   _____

   _____

   _____

   _____

4. My hero is allergic to _____

   When he gets near it he _____

   _____

   _____

   _____

   _____

5. My hero is really afraid of _____

   He is afraid of this because _____

   _____

   _____

   _____

   _____

Now that you have some idea about the likes and dislikes of your hero, write a character description.

_____

_____

_____

_____

_____

_____

_____

_____

_____

_____

_____

_____

_____

_____

_____

_____

Name _____ Date _____

But What Are They Really Like?: Character Descriptions

Details help to make a character special. For instance, Sherlock Holmes smoked a pipe and played the violin. Indiana Jones is afraid of snakes. Hercules Poirot has a funny, wax mustache he loves to play with.

Complete this list of things about your hero. What does your hero do, have, or say that makes him or her different from other heroes?

My hero's favorite food is _____

_____

My hero's favorite piece of clothing is _____

_____

My hero's favorite thing to say is " _____

_____ **"**

My hero's favorite television show is _____

_____

My hero's favorite pastime is _____

_____

My hero's hobby is _____

_____

My hero's best friend is _____

_____

Now, on a separate sheet of paper, write about a day in the life of your hero. A happy day. A fun day. A day with friends doing all the things your hero loves to do. Have your hero encounter all of the things he or she dislikes, too! Then your readers will know everything about this hero that you want them to know. Title your story:

A Day in the Life of My Hero. . .

With Friends Like This, Who Needs Fiends?: The Two-Sided Character

Robert Lewis Stevenson wrote a novel called *Dr. Jekyll and Mr. Hyde*. What is frightening about *Dr. Jekyll and Mr. Hyde* is that Dr. Jekyll is a nice guy and Mr. Hyde is horrific. But guess what? They are the same person.

Sometimes the scariest monster can be someone you trust. What if your best friend turned out to be a mole person from the center of the earth? Sure, he's nice on the surface, but he just wants your trust so he can conquer the world for the mole people.

On a separate sheet of paper, write a story about a friend who isn't who he or she seems to be. For this story, make up a friend the same way you made up a hero. Don't use a real friend as your model. (You don't want to hurt anyone's feelings. It's hard to find good friends!) Title your story:

The Friend

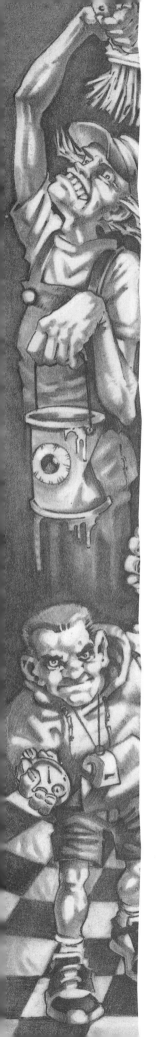

These Are a Few of My Favorite Screams: Turning What You Like into Something Scary

What do you think of when you think of horror stories? Banging shutters? Creaking doors? Vampires, witches, ghosts, and ghouls? You don't think of ice cream do you? Or candy, or playing video games, or . . .

Make a list of all of your favorite things.

_____

_____

_____

_____

_____

Now, in order to write your story, you need to create some conflict by introducing a central problem. Go back to your list of your favorite things. Choose one thing and turn it into something terrifying. That is where the problem will come from. The solution will get everything back to normal!

Let's say you choose ice cream. How can you turn loving ice cream into something terrifying? Read the following and you'll get the idea.

> There once was an evil scientist who disliked children. It was his plan to rid the world of all the children. So he created an ice cream that transformed children into popsicles for hungry aliens.

> One day after school, you and your best friend, Joey, buy two big scoops of rocky road. Joey takes a big lick when something strange starts to happen. Ice crystals form around Joey's mouth and eyes. His face turns blue. You drop your cone of rocky road and run from the ice cream store in terror. You've only run two blocks when you realize Joey is in trouble and you need to do something about it. . . .

Get the idea? Now, use a separate sheet of paper and have fun writing your story, titled:

How What I Like Became What I Fear

House of Horror Floor Plan: Where the Action Is

Hurry, hurry, step right up! Visit a house of horrors unlike any you've ever seen before. It will scare you. It will terrify you. It will make your skin crawl! And all because *you* created it. Design your very own house of horrors. Use a separate piece of paper to draw a floor plan of the house, showing where everything is going to be. Fill your house with what you find the most thrilling and terrifying. Once you have finished, on a separate sheet of paper, write a story about how you ventured into the house on a moonlit night all alone. In your story, enter on one side of the house and make your way through to the other side. When you see the things that scare you, be sure to describe how you feel and react. Use active verbs and descriptive language, too. Title your story:

My Journey to the House of Horrors

Where Was That Again?: Unexpected Locations for Horror

We all think of haunted houses as scary. They are intended to be. After all, they're haunted. But think about this. Where else can scares occur? Well, horror can happen anywhere, as you are about to discover.

For example:

A football game at school gets weird when zombies want to join the team.

A slumber party at your friend's house goes crazy when the pizza delivery man is from another planet.

An amusement park adventure takes a turn when the rides don't end.

A baseball game gets strange when the announcer hypnotizes everyone in the stadium.

Begin this exercise by writing a list of places you love to go: the mall, the movies, your friend's house, and so on.

_____

_____

_____

_____

_____

_____

_____

_____

_____

_____

_____

_____

_____

_____

Pick one of those places.

_____

Next, think of an event that occurs at the place you have chosen.

_____

_____

_____

_____

_____

_____

_____

_____

_____

_____

_____

_____

_____

_____

_____

_____

_____

_____

Now, let that event get out of control because someone or something has turned the ordinary into the bizarre. On a separate sheet of paper, write a story titled:

The Happening

The Monster Under the Bed: Where Is It and What Is It?

Have you ever avoided looking under the bed because of what you might find there? Sometimes *scary* is right under your nose. When you were little, you were probably afraid of monsters in the closet or under the bed. Now that you're older you don't believe in things like that anymore. Or do you? What if one of those monsters turned out to be real? Say that one under the bed? What would it look like? What if all that stuff you threw under the bed came to life? On a separate sheet of paper, write a story about the secret mysteries in your room venturing out to haunt you. Begin your story by describing your bedroom before you clean it. If there were a creature hidden somewhere in the depths of your room, where would it be? What are you going to do about it? Title your story:

The Scare In My Room

Write Fright, Copyright © Good Year Books.

Where in the World?: Doing Research on Location

Scary stuff happens in every corner of the globe. If you went on an imaginary trip around the world, you might encounter castle hauntings, evil leprechauns, talking skeletons, vampires, ghosts, or weird creatures. For this exercise, you are going on a scary vacation. First, choose a country you would like to visit. Next, research the country so that you can add details about the location to your tale. Research landmarks, legends, customs, and even food. Remember, research is an important part of your job as an author. You are writing about a place you have probably never been.

After researching your chosen location, write a narrative about your vacation land becoming covered by the shadow of fear. Perhaps a ghost, a ghoul, a zombie, an animal, a stranger, or even just a really mean bully could make that place seem far less relaxing. Title your story:

My Holiday With Horror

Time Was:
Adding a Touch of History

Some horror and science fiction writers use time travel as a basis for their stories. They transport readers into the distant future. Other writers write historical novels. They set scary stories in the past. History becomes the backdrop for a fictional story about the unexpected. Focus on the past, and use history in your tale. For starters, read the following story:

Peril at the Potomac

"General Washington, the troops are afraid to cross the Potomac. They say there's a giant dragon at the bottom of the river that devours anyone crossing to the other side. They refuse to even go near the water."

"If we don't attack now we will lose the element of surprise."

"But what about the monster, sir?"

"There is no monster," the general steamed.

Just then, on that cold December eve, a green scaled beast with blood-red eyes burst through the icy waters of the Potomac. Men scattered everywhere, scrambling and screaming for dear life. Only General Washington stood his ground. The dragon let forth a mighty blast of foul air from its nostrils. Washington's hair fluttered in the rank breeze. Washington set his eyes upon the being in a fixed stare. Stepping forward through the frozen mud, General Washington approached the mighty lizard. The men, from the safety of the woods, stared in amazement as their commander in chief advanced upon the enemy from the deep. Before their very eyes, they watched as General George Washington whispered to the monster and began to scratch behind the slimy creature's ears.

No one will speak of it today, and no self respecting Englishman will admit it, but that fateful day General George Washington and his rebels defeated the English Army on the banks of the Potomac while riding the back of a great green mysterious and patriotic river monster.

Now it's your turn! Choose a moment in history. Research it, filling a page with facts about the event. Then rewrite the event by adding a mysterious creature to the tale. Call your tale:

You Won't Read About This in the History Books

Write Fright, Copyright © Good Year Books.

Where the Action Is:
In the Terrible, Terrifying Sea

There's something about the sea that grips our imagination. It's a place where great white whales are swimming. It's a place where mean, ferocious sharks are searching for their prey. It is also a place of lost civilizations, mermaids, ghost ships, sunken treasures, violent storms, and weird and wonderful sea creatures. For the horror writer, it's full of wonderful ideas. Brainstorm a list of story ideas similar to the ideas above. Think about what kind of sea story you would like to write.

_____
_____
_____
_____
_____
_____
_____
_____
_____
_____
_____
_____
_____
_____
_____
_____
_____

Now, on a separate sheet of paper, write your story. Title it:

From The Depths

Asking Yourself Why: The Reason Behind the Horror

While you're creating scary stories, don't forget the underlying motives of the character's actions, the "why" of what's happening. Answer the questions below about a zombie tale. Decide for yourself why the events are occurring. It's up to you.

Zombie Invasion

1. "Zombies! Zombies!" screamed the folks in the normally quiet town of Carleton. Zombies had suddenly invaded their tiny farming community. Hundreds of zombies wandered the fields of corn, wheat, and hay. Why are there zombies in the town?

_____

_____

_____

_____

_____

_____

_____

_____

2. The zombies roam into people's houses, lay in their beds, watch television, and break things. Why?

_____

_____

_____

_____

_____

_____

_____

_____

3. One person in the town has a great plan for getting rid of the zombies. What is the plan?

_____

_____

_____

_____

_____

_____

_____

4. Unfortunately, no one trusts this person. Why?

_____

_____

_____

_____

_____

_____

_____

5. The townspeople finally agree to trust this person and try the plan. Why?

_____

_____

_____

_____

_____

_____

_____

Who's That Ghoul?: The Ghost With a Job to Do

There is something about a good ghost story that chills us to the bone. Ghost stories are mysterious and scary. For this exercise, you are going to write your own ghost story. A ghost is a character as important as any real person in your tales. They have personalities, characteristics, and motives.

Here's an idea: Write about a ghost who is haunting the house he once lived in. New owners have just moved in and notice weird goings on directly related to the job held by the former owner. For instance, let's say the ghost is Joseph Pipall, a former plumber. The faucet turns itself on, they hear the sound of wrenches, and the owners think they see a tool belt floating through the air. They hear a voice muttering, "The pipes are rusty." The ghost won't leave the house until the pipes have been replaced. Or let's say your ghost is a former clothes designer, Lady Susan Demure. Mannequins move on their own, a sewing machine is heard at odd hours, and the new owners' clothing is redesigned while they sleep.

Build suspense by unfolding the mystery of who the ghost is. Before you begin your tale, brainstorm a list of character names and fun jobs.

Character's name	Character's former job
_____	_____
_____	_____
_____	_____
_____	_____
_____	_____
_____	_____
_____	_____
_____	_____

Now, on a separate sheet of paper, write your ghostly tale.

Chapter Four

Styles of Suspense: Story Starters

Objectives

- To help students examine familiar story forms and how changing different elements in these forms can create new horror stories.
- To incorporate language skills in slightly more complex writing assignments.
- To allow students to write their own stories with the help of specific story starters.

Suggestions for Success

Encourage students to use previously mastered skills in their creative writing.

The exercises titled "Professor Canard's Experiment" can be done in or out of order. They are all story starter ideas about transformations. Although they are written in sequence, they are easily understood as self-contained exercises.

Enrichment Ideas

Have your class read "The Monkey's Paw."

Many of the exercises in this chapter utilize different literary genres for story ideas. They are intended as inspiration and to spark the imagination. Students may need assistance in brainstorming story ideas before they begin writing their tales.

Demeter's Arbor: Using Mythology for Ideas and Story Structure

Read this Greek myth, titled "Demeter's Arbor."

Once there was a young prince who came across a beautiful arbor of magnificent trees. "These trees would make a wonderful dining hall for my palace," he thought. The next day he returned with a party of soldiers to chop down the trees. Just as they lifted their axes, an old woman appeared.

"This is my mistress's wood," she exclaimed. "She would not like you chopping down her trees." The soldiers placed their axes on the ground. The young prince smiled. "I do not fear your mistress. I need wood for my dining hall and these are the finest trees I have ever seen." He raised his ax and the old woman revealed herself to be Demeter, Goddess of the Earth. "You are right," she nodded. "If you believe your dining hall is more important than my arbor, go ahead and chop. But from this day forward you will always be hungry."

The Prince laughed. "I am not afraid of your magic." Demeter did not hear him because she had disappeared with the wind. When the young prince returned home, he soon discovered how real her magic was. He ate and ate and ate but no matter how much he ate, he could never get enough. His family was forced to turn him out of the house. His friends could not help him because when he came to visit, he ate so much they soon ran out of food. The young prince found himself out on the streets, searching and begging for food. One day he was so fiercely hungry, in his desperation he devoured himself. And that was the end of the young prince forever.

Turn this story into a modern scary story of your own. Use the ideas in the tale, but give them a modern twist.

Write Fright, Copyright © Good Year Books.

Get Mythed:
Looking to Mythology for Ideas

Many horror story writers use mythology and folk tales in their writing. For example, the story of Frankenstein is based upon the myth of Prometheus. As a horror author, mythology and folk tales can provide *you* with ideas. Research two of the following Greek myths: Medusa, Sysiphus, Icarus, Midas, Pygmalion, Orpheus, Pegasus and Chimera, Echo and Narcissus. Fill a page with notes about each story. Then, use your notes to help you write a modern horror story based on the myth you find more interesting. Use a separate sheet of paper.

Modeling "The Monkey's Paw": Creating Your Own Classic

The story of "The Monkey's Paw" is a classic in horror literature. A family is granted three wishes by a magical monkey's paw. The family soon discovers that wishes can go very wrong. There are many other folk tales and stories about wishes that go afoul. In these stories, the characters get their wishes, but not exactly the way they intended!

Make a list of things someone could wish for.

_____
_____
_____
_____
_____
_____
_____
_____
_____
_____
_____
_____
_____
_____
_____
_____
_____
_____
_____
_____

Write some notes about how the wishes could go wrong.

_____

_____

_____

_____

_____

_____

_____

_____

_____

_____

_____

_____

_____

_____

_____

_____

_____

_____

_____

_____

_____

_____

_____

_____

_____

_____

_____

_____

_____

Now, on a separate sheet of paper, write a story about a character that makes one of the wishes. How does the wish go wrong? What does the main character do to make things right again?

Let the Punishment Fit the Crime: Bad Behavior Can Make for a Great Story

Sometimes bad behavior becomes its own punishment. Here are two examples, one ancient and one modern. In the Greek myth of "Demeter's Arbor," the prince considers his dining hall more important than Demeter's trees. Demeter punishes him by making food and eating destructive elements in his life. In the movie <u>Liar, Liar,</u> the father lies all the time. His son wishes his father has to tell the truth and nothing but the truth for a whole day.

Make a list of bad behaviors:

_____

_____

_____

_____

_____

_____

_____

_____

_____

_____

_____

_____

_____

_____

_____

_____

_____

Now start a story about a character with one of the bad behaviors on your list. Describe your character, too. What are his likes and dislikes? Who are his friends? What do his friends think about his bad behavior?

_____

_____

_____

_____

_____

_____

_____

_____

_____

_____

_____

_____

_____

_____

_____

_____

_____

_____

_____

_____

_____

_____

_____

Now something happens! Your character's bad behavior is turned against him. Either he can no longer act the way he always has or he has to act that way all the time. Maybe everyone starts behaving badly in the same way toward your character. Let the behavior get out of control. How does the character stop these events from continuing?

The Beast Next Door:
Favorite Tales Can Be Scary, Too!

Sometimes all you need to do to make a folk or fairy tale terrifying is to bring it up to date. What if there were a beast like the character in "Beauty in the Beast" living in your neighborhood? Or what if you were walking in the woods and came across a bizarre gingerbread house? What if you met three bears who owned a house and talked? The possibilities are endless, so let's get started. To begin, write a list of your favorite folk tales and fairy tales.

_____

_____

_____

_____

_____

_____

_____

_____

_____

_____

_____

_____

_____

_____

_____

_____

Now, on a separate sheet of paper, choose one tale. Rewrite it as a modern tale of terror.

Petrifying Parables, Part I: Messages Well-Taken

Parables are short stories that have a message or moral. Many tales of horror also contain a message or moral about behavior. Read this classic tale. Then write a tale of terror based on the story.

The Boy Who Cried Wolf

There once was a boy whose job it was to tend all the sheep for his town. It was a very important job, but he didn't like it. He was always bored. So, to pass the time, he decided to cry wolf to see what would happen.

"Wolf! Wolf!" he shouted. Everyone came running to save the sheep from the wolf. The boy laughed at them. The townspeople scolded him and went back about their business. After a while the boy became bored again and decided to try his trick.

"Wolf! Wolf!" he screamed. Everyone came running to save the sheep from the wolf. The boy laughed at them. Now the townspeople lost their patience. "If you continue to play this little game," they said, "the next time we will not come." The boy just laughed. He took no heed to their warning.

Shortly after the townspeople left, sure enough, a real wolf slinked out from between two trees. He had been waiting for everyone to leave. The boy cried, "Wolf! Wolf!" but no one came. "Wolf! Wolf!" he screamed. "I really mean it this time." But everyone was tired of his game. No one came to save the little boy. He was never seen or heard from again.

Write your own story based upon the tale of the boy who cried wolf. Your story could be about a girl who cries "Ghost!" or a boy who screams "Leave me alone!" Brainstorm a list of possible plots for your story.

_____

_____

_____

_____

Now, on a separate sheet of paper, write your tale of terror. Refer back to "The Boy Who Cried Wolf" as you need to!

Petrifying Parables, Part Two:
The Lion and the Mouse

Read this classic story.

The Lion and the Mouse

One day, a mouse was running home with a kernel of corn in his mouth when he ran right into a lion. The lion grabbed the tiny mouse with his gigantic paw and said, "My, my! What have we here? A little snack for after my nap. How nice."

The mouse, terrified, pleaded with the mighty lion. "Oh, please Mr. Lion," he said. "If you spare me now, I promise some day I will do a good deed for you."

The lion roared with laughter. "How can you, a tiny mouse, do a good deed for me, a mighty lion? That is the funniest thing I have ever heard. But I will let you go because you have made me laugh so hard. Now run home, tiny mouse, before I change my mind." The tiny mouse ran home, grateful to the lion.

The next day, the mouse was out foraging for food when he saw the mighty lion trapped in a hunter's snare. The lion was shaking with terror.

"Ahuh!" The mouse grinned. "I knew I would be able to do you a good deed one day. I will free you from this trap." The mouse climbed up onto the snare and chewed away the knots that kept the lion prisoner. Soon the lion fell free from the trap. He thanked the mouse. He was grateful to be free. Later, when the hunters came to gather up the lion, they found their net broken and empty. They noticed little teeth marks on the snare and shook their heads. As for the mouse, he had a tale to tell when he went home.

On a separate sheet of paper, write a scary story based upon this tale of one good deed deserving another. Your tale could be about a meeting with any kind of creepy character and how you help each other.

Story Inspiration: Fear Inducing Phrases

Choose one of the expressions below. Then use that expression as the main theme of your story. Be sure to answer the five main questions of good writing: <u>who</u>, <u>what</u>, <u>where</u>, <u>when</u>, and <u>why</u>. Write your story on a separate sheet of paper. Use the expression as your title.

1. **Let sleeping dogs lie.**

2. **Look before you leap.**

3. **New dangers can make you forget old ones.**

4. **He is just a wolf in sheep's clothing.**

Professor Canard's Experiment #1: A Startling Change

Your science teacher, Professor John Canard, has been locked away in his laboratory working on an experiment for days now. You go to visit him to find out why he hasn't been to school all week when he eagerly invites you to join him in his laboratory as he tests his latest discovery: a drink that tastes like ginger ale but looks like hot cocoa. Carefully, you sip from the mug of hot steamy sludge. It does taste like ginger ale and slides down your throat. Suddenly, you realize that this newest experiment of Professor Canard's is not just a new ginger ale. You feel your skin start to crawl. Your hair is standing on end. Your fingernails are twitching. You are turning into a gigantic grasshopper. You feel different, you look different, and all of a sudden you have a great urge to hop outside and into the grass.

On a separate sheet of paper, write a story about your adventures as a giant grasshopper. Title it:

Diary of a Student Grasshopper

Professor Canard's Experiment #2: Bigger Than Life

You hop into Professor John Canard's office. Your forearms twitch. You try to speak, but try as you might, no words come. You are still a giant, upset grasshopper. "I am so sorry." Professor Canard cowers in the corner, terrified by the sight of you. "I had no idea my experiment would do anything like that. Please forgive me." You grab a piece of chalk with your pinchers and start to write on the blackboard. "Change me back!"

Professor Canard reads what you have written and goes to his desk. He takes out a small vial of liquid and pours it into a glass of water. "Drink this." He hands you the glass and you sip it down a little at a time. Suddenly, a change takes place. Your muscles twitch. You feel like hopping. In an explosion of insect vigor you burst out of your grasshopper shell.

You are once again you. What a relief! That is until you feel a jolt of energy surge through you. Your body shakes and everything inside you is bumping around. You are growing, bigger, bigger. "Professor, what's happening to me?" You panic. "Professor!" The ceiling is getting closer. You are about to bump your head.

"This shouldn't be happening," the professor cries out. Your head bursts through the roof of the building. You continue to grow. Your muscles are bulging and you are towering over everyone. People are running from you and screaming.

On a separate sheet of paper, write a story about being a giant titled:

The Jumbo, Gigantic Creature is Me

Professor Canard's Experiment #3: A Small World

"All right Professor John Canard!" you bellow, high above his shattered office. "I have had enough of this nonsense. I want to be myself again!" You grab the professor by the collar as he tries to run away. He screams as you lift him to your face. Just then you feel a pin prick in your pinky. The professor has stabbed you with a hypodermic needle. Before you know it, you're shrinking. Life is returning to the unremarkable. Then you realize that things are getting big. You are continuing to shrink, smaller and smaller. Soon you are the size of an ant. You run from the office screaming. You find yourself outside in the giant world of humans stomping everywhere.

On a separate sheet of paper, write a story about being as small as an ant. Title it:

The Ant Transformation

Professor Canard's Experiment #4: Caught in the Web

Professor John Canard is looking into his microscope at a blood sample. After a very rough day, you make your way back to his office. You're determined to have him fix you this time. Finally, after hours of climbing, you reach the plateau. You are standing on the slide. Above you is a mammoth eyeball gazing down. You wave your hands and Professor Canard realizes it's you. Carefully, he takes you on the slide across the room.

"I am so sorry, my friend. I'll just put you under this Randomatic Laser and turn you back to normal size."

He places you under a large laser.

"First," he says, "I must make some adjustments on the computer." He runs to the computer and types in commands. "Oh no! I don't want the Internet." He hits a key. A burst of blue light streams from the laser. The light pulses through you. The room disappears. Suddenly you find yourself standing in the midst of the strangest city you have ever seen. A city of the future.

Wait a minute! This isn't a city. This is the logic board of Professor Canard's computer. You are inside the computer! A mighty surge of power grabs you and pulls from the microchip you are standing on. It is pulling you down a tube and into the World Wide Web.

On a separate sheet of paper, write a story about being inside a machine.

Professor Canard's Experiment #5: A Petrifying Parent

After a week traveling the World Wide Web, you finally find your way home. That's right, home. To mom. After searching through e-mail connections for a week, you finally are able to send a message to your mom. Now she is headed for Professor Canard's office with a print out of your face with a message . . . HELP!

"I want my child back and now!" she says to him.

"Of course," Professor Canard says calmly. "Let's see what we can do."

He sits at his computer and enters an address into the World Wide Web, drawing you into his computer. Then, turning on the laser, Professor Canard finally brings you back into the real world as a real person.

At last you're back to normal!

You and your mom thank Professor Canard and are about to leave when someone accidentally turns on the Randomatic Laser. A blast hits your mom and she is paralyzed with fear. Before you or the professor can turn off the laser, your mother is bigger than a 10-story skyscraper and boy is she mad.

On a separate sheet of paper, write a story about having a gigantic mom. Title it:

The Larger Than Life Mom

Professor Canard's Experiment #6: A Monstrous, Creepy, Crawly Problem

"All right Professor John Canard!" your mom bellows, high above his shattered office. "I have had enough of this nonsense. I want to be a normal mom."

This time the professor reverses the polarity on the Randomatic Laser. Your mom is back to the way she was—with no side effects at all. Everyone sighs, especially you.

As you go to leave, one of the construction workers spills another one of Professor Canard's experiments. Blue liquid sizzles into the floorboards and disappears. Everyone stares in disbelief, waiting and wondering what is going to happen. Before long, the floorboards burst forth and out crawls an army of gargantuan bugs—monstrous spiders dripping venom, colossal ants looking for lunch. And a goliath beetle with its eyes on you.

On a separate sheet of paper, write a story about enormous bugs attacking your town titled:

The Town That Was Really Bugged

Where Am I?: Lost in the Story

Have you ever gone for a walk, only to find yourself in another neighborhood you didn't recognize? You had no idea how you got there or how to get home! Sometimes being lost can be the scariest thing in the world. Things that would never bother or scare you seem more foreboding and terrifying than ever.

Being lost can be a great start for a scary story. Perhaps you wandered into a parallel universe where everything looks right but really is all wrong. Or maybe you walked through a door into another land like Oz or Narnia and you keep returning to the same spot.

On a separate sheet of paper, write a story about being lost. Think of how you got lost. Then try to find your way home. What happens? Title your story:

Lost!

War of the Words: Creating a Scene

H. G. Wells wrote a famous book called *War of the Worlds* about a Martian invasion. In 1938, Orson Welles created a radio play based on the book. The play was designed to sound like a real news broadcast. The show was so realistic that people all across America truly believed the world was being invaded by Martians and went into a panic. Once they realized it was a radio play, they were relieved—but upset.

For this exercise, on a separate sheet of paper, write your own radio play. The dialogue should be realistic. Make it sound like a real news broadcast. Will listeners mistake it for a real event?

You may want to listen to the original "War of the Worlds" broadcast. You can find it at your local library.

Chapter Five

Don't Be Afraid to Change: Rewriting Ideas

Objectives

- To have students rewrite a story using a variety of different rewriting techniques and storytelling approaches.
- To encourage students to improve writing skills by reviewing finished work and rewriting.
- To enable students to learn there are many different ways to tell the same story.
- To help students see that different approaches to the same story can highlight different aspects of the story and change its focus.

Strategies for Success

Choose stories for rewriting from the collection of stories that your students have written throughout the year. You may also wish to use these exercises directly following any of the story-writing exercises. They are designed to focus the students on rewriting, editing, and revising. Students will find these three skills extremely useful when applied to different story assignments.

Discuss with the class how rewriting is a method used by all writers to improve their work. It is not a punishment for authors of bad stories.

Have everyone pick one of their stories for rewriting and have them choose some of the rewriting techniques to apply to their story.

Enrichment Ideas

Encourage rewriting by dividing your students into groups. Have them read their stories aloud and offer constructive suggestions for improving their tales.

Have students examine and discuss how different authors begin and end their tales. What are students' thoughts on why the authors made the choices they did?

Schedule rewriting "clinics" during which students can edit and revise their tales.

Write Fright, Copyright © Good Year Books.

Where Do I Begin?:
Starting the Story Sensationally

Some stories start at the beginning of the action.

> **For example:**
>
> It was a quiet morning in Cheeriville when the aliens landed.

Some stories start right in middle of all the action.

> **For example:**
>
> The vampire was closing in on us. There seemed no way out . . .

Some stories start with a premonition of things to come.

> **For example:**
>
> Joe always hated spiders. Sure, this one was tiny, but still it scared him.

Some stories start at the end of the action and work their way back.

> **For example:**
>
> It was quiet now, but Sarah knew she would never be the same again, not after killing the monster.

Where you start *your* story will tell your readers what you think the story is about. If you start at the beginning of the action, with a quiet town and a normal day, we know something has to change. But what? Readers have to wait to find out. If you start with a premonition, readers will know that during the story Joe will have to face his fear of spiders. If you start in the middle or at the end of the action, you have to find the time to go back and tell readers what happened.

Choose a story that you have written. Using a separate sheet of paper, write a new beginning using one of the techniques described above. Continue rewriting your tale with this new approach. How does your new beginning change the rest of the story?

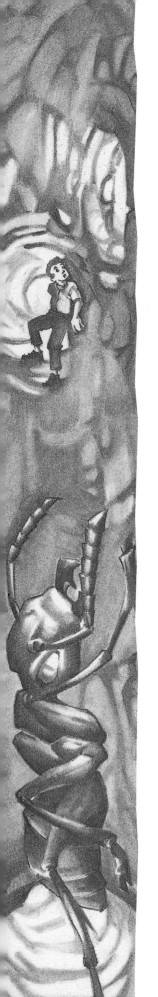

Character Rewrites: Creating Complete Lives

When you rewrite, it is a good idea to go through your story to see if all of your characters are strong. Not all the characters need to be as strong as the hero or antagonist, but they should be able to stand out in a crowd.

One of the best ways of clarifying a character is to write his or her biography, fleshing out the details of the character's life. Answer the following questions about a character in one of your tales.

1. **Where was your character born?**

   _____

   _____

   _____

   _____

2. **What is your character's family like?**

   _____

   _____

   _____

   _____

3. **Does your character have brothers or sisters?**

   _____

   _____

   _____

   _____

4. **If so, what are their names?**

   _____

   _____

   _____

5. What are they like?

_____

_____

_____

_____

6. Do all of the family members get along?

_____

_____

_____

_____

7. What are your character's hobbies?

_____

_____

_____

_____

8. What kind of school did your character go to?

_____

_____

_____

_____

9. What does your character like about school?

_____

_____

_____

_____

10. What does your character look like?

_____

_____

_____

_____

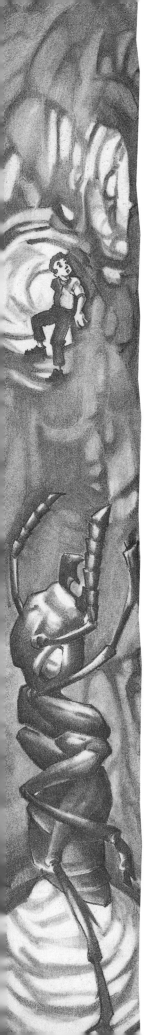

11. What are your character's favorite foods?

_____

_____

_____

_____

12. What are your character's hobbies?

_____

_____

_____

_____

13. What things really bug your character?

_____

_____

_____

_____

14. What kind of clothes does your character wear?

_____

_____

_____

_____

15. What is your character's favorite music?

_____

_____

_____

_____

The Scary Ending: Take Their Breath Away

Changing the ending of a story adds an extra kick that makes scary stories more fun. You, the writer, have lots of endings to choose from.

The happy ending: All's well that ends well. Everyone is happy. Nothing wrong with that.

The happy ending with a wink: You think you killed the monster and you did. But somehow, you let readers know there is another monster waiting to rear its ugly head. Perhaps the monster had a baby. Or maybe someone in the family has become a monster without anybody knowing. This ending suggests a sequel.

The unhappy ending: The hero is defeated and the monster rules the world. Or does it? This ending also suggests a sequel.

The happy ending with just a twitch of terror left behind: This ending suggests that all is well but that the characters will never be the same again. And why should they be the same if they lived through a horror story?

The no ending ending: This is like the nightmare that never ends. Readers keep coming back to the beginning or the middle. This ending can be very scary in the right story.

Using a separate sheet of paper, choose one of your stories and write a new ending using one of the techniques described above. Does your new ending change the rest of the story?

Point of View: Changing Perspective

The viewpoint an author uses in a story tells a lot about the story itself. There are four types of viewpoints that an author can use in a story.

omniscient: told in the third person by a narrator who knows all the thoughts and actions of all the characters

limited omniscient: told in the third person, limited to the thoughts and views of one character

first person: told by one person who is usually the narrator or main character; uses first-person pronouns

objective: told in the first person, but somewhat like a reporter; does not tell what characters think or feel or what to think about the actions of the story

Using a separate sheet of paper, choose one of your stories and change the point of view. For example, if your story is a first-person narrative, tell it in the objective point of view. Make sure you keep the point of view consistent throughout your tale.

Suggested Reading

There are many books out there for young readers in the horror genre. Naturally, the first series that comes to mind is the *Goosebumps* series by R. L. Stine, published by Scholastic Paperback. There are plenty to choose from. They are fast reads and fine examples for studying story structure.

R. L. Stine has written another horror series, *Fear Street*, published by Archway Paperback. This series is for older readers.

Alfred Hitchcock's collections of short stories for young readers, published by Random House, offers some wonderful stories by some of this century's best writers: Daphne du Maurier, Agatha Christie, Joseph Conrad, and Roald Dahl—one of Hitchcock's favorite writers.

Although Roald Dahl is not technically a horror writer, most of his books feature story elements commonly found in the horror genre. Some examples are the sympathetic monster or monsters in *James and The Giant Peach,* published by Puffin Paperback, characters being punished for their excesses in *Charlie and the Chocolate Factory,* published by Puffin Paperback, or a child with telekinetic powers in *Matilda,* published by Puffin Paperback. Then there is also the straight horror story—*The Witches,* published by Puffin Paperback.

Bruce Coville has written two engaging series of books, one called the *Camp Haunted Hills* series and the other, the *My Teacher Is An Alien* series, both available from Minstrel Books.

Mary Blount Christian's *Swamp Monsters,* published by Puffin, is a fine example of turning a tale around and making the monsters the heroes.

John Bellairs' *House with a Clock in its Walls* trilogy, published by Puffin Paperback, is a series filled with mystery and suspense.

Another good series is the *Animorphs* by K. A. Applegate, published by Scholastic Books. Although the *Animorphs* series is not specifically horror, but more sci-fi in genre, it does feature frightening monsters.

Deborah and James Howe's *Bunnicula: A Rabbit Tale of Mystery,* published by Aladdin Paperback, features Harold the dog and Chester the cat, who believe the newest member of their household, Bunnicula, named after Dracula, is a vampire.

Also noteworthy are Zilpha Keatley Snyder's *The Egypt Game,* published by Yearling paperback, Elizabeth George Speare's *The Witch of Blackbird Pond,* published by Yearling paperback, and Alvin Schwartz's books *Scary Stories to Tell In The Dark: Collected From American Folklore, More Scary Stories,* and *Scary Stories 3: More Tales To Chill Your Bones,* published in paperback by Harper Trophy.

Christopher Pike and Joan Lowery Nixon have both written many horror genre books for advanced younger readers.

There are also quite a few excellent ghost stories in more modern story collections. Have students read Mark Twain's "The Girl with the Golden Arm" and stories in books such as Maria Leach's *The Thing At The Foot Of The Bed and Other Scary Tales*. There are many exclusively scary story collections in the school and local library and bookstores for students to choose from.

As a class project, you may want your students to write book reports about horror stories to share with the class. You may also want to start a horror corner with its own library.

About the Authors

Mark Pierce is the program manager of The Homeless Education Program For Dallas Public Schools and a dedicated teacher. Karen Jennings is a stand-up comedian, actor, and educator. Together they are the authors of *Let The Laughs Begin: Humor Writing in the Classroom* and *Storytelling Tips and Tales*, both for Good Year Books. They live in Dallas, Texas with their baby son Casey and two dogs, Buster and Chapin. They enjoy scaring each other by writing together.